Original title:
The Houseplant Haiku

Copyright © 2025 Creative Arts Management OÜ
All rights reserved.

Author: Miriam Kensington
ISBN HARDBACK: 978-1-80581-750-5
ISBN PAPERBACK: 978-1-80581-277-7
ISBN EBOOK: 978-1-80581-750-5

Tiny Oasis in a Corner

In a pot, so small,
A rogue fern takes its stand.
Whispers of drama,
With a cactus keeping watch.

Sunlight pours like gossip,
Leaves raise eyebrows high.
Did the spider plant just flirt?
Nature's soap opera thrives.

Nature's Quiet Confidant

The rubber tree listens,
To secrets in the night.
Tales of lost socks and snacks,
Under soft moonlight's glow.

Its leaves nod, full of wisdom,
Rooted, it won't freak out.
Who needs therapy anyway?
When you have a houseplant!

Shadows of Serenity

Succulent in the sun,
With a grin, it stretches wide.
Cousin to the chill vibes,
Waves at the passing cat.

A picture of calm chaos,
Petals hide the madness.
In its green, we find peace,
Except when it starts to droop.

Cultivating Calm

Watered with affection,
Tiny leaves say, 'Thanks, dude!'
Staring at a grow light,
Dreaming of jungle fame.

Dancing in the wind,
Potted plant shows its moves.
Next up, a TikTok star,
With charisma made of green!

Essence of Earth Within

Leaves like little umbrellas,
Hiding from the dust bunnies,
I water them with purpose,
But they just want more sun!

With each droop they remind me,
Of my own lack of sleep,
Yet they thrive on my neglect,
Guess I'm not a total creep!

Harmony in the Humble

Pothos, you green master,
And I, your lowly slave,
You feast on my errors,
While I quietly wave.

Each leaf a tiny soldier,
In my room's green brigade,
I sip coffee with pride,
As you unleash your shade.

Rooted in Reverie

In a pot aged like fine wine,
Sits a cactus with a sneer,
You prick, I laugh, it's not a crime,
I'll never volunteer!

Succulents give sly winks,
As I forget to feed,
Yet they live without a care,
I wish I could succeed!

Green Dreams in the Living Room

Ferns dance in breezy bliss,
While I tripped on their fronds,
I laugh, they sway and hiss,
Who said plants can't respond?

Tiny pots across the shelf,
Whisper secrets in the night,
I wonder if they know me,
In their leafy delight!

Sunlit Sanctuary

In a pot, it sits proud,
Receiving rays of bright sun,
Whispering to the dust,
"I think I've found my home!"

Leafy fingers stretch wide,
Claiming space on the table,
Clusters of green giggles,
As cats plot their next leap.

Woven Life

Spider plant's long whispers,
Sharing tales of the moon,
"Did you see that watering?"
"They drown me like a cartoon!"

Spider lilies eyeing pots,
Gossip of ferns and weeds,
"She thinks she's the best here,"
But her stems are full of seeds.

Harmony in Stillness

Stillness in the green room,
Socks on their tiny feet,
Cacti throw gentle shade,
"We're all just here to eat!"

Peace in every leaf's sway,
A dance of joy and care,
We sip on light and love,
As dust bunnies take their share.

Ferns and Fables

Ferns perch on the windowsill,
Telling tales of the past,
"We survived all the frost,
While you lost your lunch fast!"

Their fronds unfurl with pride,
While I find my way home,
In a land of bright green,
Where even weeds can roam.

Window Silhouette

In sun's warm embrace,
A cactus strikes a pose,
Looking like a star,
In a pot, it knows.

Dust motes dance around,
Green leaves wave hello,
Trapped in glass confines,
It's a sunny show.

When shadows come near,
It plays peek-a-boo,
A plant's secret life,
In the light, so true.

On a sleepy day,
A fern dreams of flight,
Wind's a gentle friend,
In its leafy plight.

A Leaf's Soliloquy

Oh, life is so grand,
With water and light,
I stretch out my limbs,
    Hoping for a bite.

Do I look like salad?
I ponder with glee,
Why do humans munch,
On what's green like me?

Each vein tells a tale
Of sun, fun, and rain,
With a twirl and a sway,
    I forget my pain.

When the cat walks by,
I shiver in fear,
Am I just a snack,
To this furry seer?

Musical Growth

In rhythm we sway,
The plants and I sing,
A chorus of green,
With the joy we bring.

The spider plant hums,
While the vines duck and dive,
A melody grows,
Keeping all of us alive.

Cacti clap their arms,
In a desert-like beat,
The philodendron sways,
To the drum of the heat.

Together they dance,
And we giggle with cheer,
A leafy ballet,
In our little sphere.

Whispering Leaves

Oh, secrets they tell,
On a breezy day,
With a rustle and sigh,
They gossip and sway.

A succulent grins,
With a wink and a twist,
Saying, "Stay hydrated!"
As it laughs at the mist.

When the morning comes,
They stretch and they yawn,
In a leafy ballet,
By the first light of dawn.

"Don't forget to chat!"
Says the jade with a grin,
For friends are the roots,
That help laughter begin.

Blooms of Reflection

In the pot they stare,
Each leaf a funny face,
Roots dance in warm air,
Making their home a place.

Sunlight spills like gold,
Green thumbs tap their feet,
Stories left untold,
As dirt clumps form a seat.

Smiles in Succulents

Plump and almost round,
They giggle in the light,
Water's joy is found,
In bursts of colors bright.

With spines like tiny guards,
They hold their ground with pride,
Playing their green cards,
In the sunshine they abide.

Fragrant Recollections

Herbs whisper of spice,
Basil's giggle pervades,
Mint takes a swish, oh nice,
As laughter gently fades.

Each leaf a playful jest,
Brewing memories sweet,
Time for tea and rest,
In pots with roots so neat.

The Caretaker's Touch

With watering can high,
They dance in the night air,
Laughter fills the sky,
Plants sway without a care.

Each time the shears clip,
A leaf falls with a grin,
They're ready for the trip,
In the sun, they always win.

Growing with Grace

In a pot, I bloom bright,
Trying hard not to fight.
Water me, love me so,
Watch my happiness grow!

Leaves reaching for the sun,
Photosynthesis fun!
A green thumb is the key,
To keep me wild and free.

The Heart of a Plant

A cactus with a grin,
Prickly but lets me in.
Throw a party on the shelf,
I'll invite the worms myself!

Succulent and quite proud,
I sing beneath the cloud.
Dancing in the sunlight,
We laugh with pure delight!

Sheltered Growth

In my cozy little nook,
I'm more than just a book.
With soil and love I thrive,
It's great to be alive!

Though dust bunnies may loom,
I'll grow amidst the gloom.
Fungi will join in the fun,
A party that's never done!

Gentle Giants

Fern fronds waving hello,
With every breeze, they glow.
Banana peels on the floor,
Who knew plants could eat more?

Large leaves shade the chair,
All my worries, they tear.
Sipping sunlight with grace,
In this happy green space!

Green Guardians

In pots they reside,
Watching me go by,
With leaves on their sides,
They seem to sigh.

When watered too much,
They turn a bit sad,
A droopy touch,
It's truly quite bad.

Yet give them some sun,
They perk up with glee,
Just like little ones,
Jumping with glee.

Late night, they conspire,
Whispering their dreams,
Plotting wild desires,
In moonlight's beams.

Life Among Leaves

In pots on my shelf,
They dance with delight,
Talking to themselves,
All through the night.

A cactus so proud,
Just poked my arm,
Says it won't back down,
It means no harm.

Spider plant, so sly,
Spinning its web,
Waiting for a fly,
Oh, plant-ly ebb.

Lettuce craves some jokes,
Says life's a salad,
Be leaf, no hoax,
It's all just valid.

Nature at Home

Fern fronds gently sway,
In the morning light,
Sending a bouquet,
Of pure delight.

A little pot says,
"Your care's a bit rough!"
I try to impress,
But it's kind of tough.

Pothos on patrol,
Keeping watchful eyes,
Fallen leaves, a scroll,
Of leafy goodbyes.

An orchid with style,
Debates with a fern,
Who's wearing it wild,
Each twist and turn!

Indoor Wilderness

Amidst a jungle scene,
A lizard will peek,
Lost in my green dream,
It's funny and sleek.

A sage with a grin,
Claims it's a wise guy,
Making my head spin,
Oh me, oh my!

Bamboo grows tall,
Stretching for the sun,
Whispers to us all,
"Don't overrun!"

So here in my house,
Plants chatter and play,
In this cozy douse,
They brighten my day.

Green Thumb Whispers

I watered my plant,
A splash in my face,
Now it's a wet joke,
In this leafy space.

It grew overnight,
Thought I heard it snore,
Was that a leaf scream?
Or a potted roar?

A cactus played dead,
With thorns on display,
I swear it's a prank,
In its own spiky way.

The fern's in a mood,
It sways with a pout,
I can't even tell,
What it's fussing about.

Petals and Ponderings

A rose with a wink,
Gossiping with bees,
They roll their small eyes,
As I plead, "Just please!"

The daisies chuckle,
At my watering can,
"Just don't drown the roots!",
That's their number one plan.

A succulent smirks,
In the sunlight's dance,
"Too much love, my friend,
Will lead to mischance!"

Violets in a row,
Sway soft in the breeze,
Plotting a takeover,
Of all of my keys.

Verdant Dreams in Sunlight

Potted parade here,
Ferns twirling around,
I caught one mid-flip,
On the living room ground.

A rogue spider plant,
With ambitions too high,
Is dangling and swaying,
Just to reach for the sky.

The choicest of leaves,
Got caught in a chat,
They're dishing like queens,
On the brash little cat.

I laugh as they bicker,
With sunshine and glee,
Who knew green could talk?
It's quite the TV!

Rooted Reflections

In the corner, a jade,
With emerald pride,
Keeps giving me looks,
Like it knows what I hide.

A bamboo once said,
"I'm taller than you!",
I snickered and thought,
"Let's see how you do!"

The pothos is sly,
With its trails like a maze,
It trips me for fun,
In its leafy craze.

Rooted companions,
Ripe humor, and charm,
Among heavenly green,
Who needs a farm?

Sips of Sun and Soil

A green friend sips light,
Leaves up high, roots below,
Caffeine for the roots,
With coffee on a plate.

Sunshine on a plate,
Watering can in hand,
Plant throws a party,
Dancing in the window.

Chasing after rays,
Photosynthesizing,
Cacti with a grin,
Succulents sing along.

Plant jokes sprout up,
'Why is it so hard grown?'
Just needs a little sun,
And a tiny dose of fun!

The Language of Leaves

Whispering in green,
Leaves gossip on the breeze,
'Is it watering time?'
'Should we throw a shindig?'

Foliage in a chat,
Talking dirt and sunshine,
Telling tales of soil,
Waging wars on the bugs.

Petals make a scene,
Vanilla-scented cares,
Plants with fashion flair,
Attire made of sunlight.

Green thumbs share a jest,
'Is that your best disguise?'
A fern in a hat now,
Sipping tea on a shelf.

Tranquil Tendrils

Tendrils gently sway,
Dancing to the warm breeze,
A song of stillness,
Peaceful in a green world.

Creeping on the wall,
Climbing up to the light,
'Just grab my hand, friend!'
'There's a dance party here!'

Amidst pots we grill,
'What's on the menu tonight?'
A taste of sunshine,
Flavored with a good laugh.

'Why is it so quiet?'
The plants just nod and wink,
They know what's coming,
A raucous garden ball!

Calm in a Pot

Nestled in their pots,
Breathe in life, sip on stars,
With a smile of green,
They hold their breath with grace.

Calm amidst the buzz,
Silent whispers of joy,
Plant jokes in the air,
'What's up with the soil?'

A curious little sprout,
Grows a giggle or two,
Rustling through the mess,
Of dirt and silly dreams.

Life in tender green,
Cherishing the breezy shift,
Fertilized with fun,
Awakening the night.

The Rhythm of Roots

Beneath the soil,
A dance of tiny roots,
They twist and they twirl,
Seeking snacks in the gloom.

In pots they reside,
Basking under bright lights,
Whispering secrets,
To those who just pass by.

Swaying with a breeze,
They flaunt their leafy pride,
Yet when I forget,
To water, they merely sigh.

Each pot holds a tale,
Of neglect and much love,
Their laughter resounds,
When I finally come home.

Overhanging Memories

A fern on the shelf,
Remembers the old days,
With each floppy leaf,
It tells of my cat's ways.

Naps by the window,
A spider plant giggles,
As dust bunnies dance,
In its hanging wiggles.

The philodendron,
Stretched out in delight,
Thinks it's a model,
With leaves glowing bright.

Caught in the sun,
They throw shade at my past,
Loyal companions,
From first bloom to the last.

Resilient Companions

Cacti hold their ground,
Spines sharp like their wit,
In dry desert air,
They sagely just sit.

Pothos vines in knots,
Climb the walls like they're pros,
Exjoking with ease,
Their arrogance shows.

A peace lily laughs,
At my worry and care,
With petals so pure,
And a scent that's quite rare.

When I leave for days,
They watch and conspire,
Plotting the return,
Of my absent desire.

Earthy Reflections

A pot on the porch,
Soil dreams of a feast,
While I sip my tea,
It lusts for a beast.

Sassy little herbs,
With flavors so bold,
Whispering sweet lies,
'We're worth more than gold!'

As I prune a sprout,
It giggles with glee,
Hoping for the day,
That it's bigger than me!

In this leafy life,
We share all our quirks,
With roots intertwined,
And a garden of smirks.

Green Heartbeat

In a pot they sway,
Little leaves dance away.
I swear they talk back,
When I miss my snack.

Sunlight beams down bright,
Photosynthesize right.
Plant parties are wild,
Nature's cheerful child.

Water them with flair,
Sneak a sip here and there.
They thirst for my jokes,
And giggle like folks.

Indoor Ecosystems

Tiny jungle vibes,
Making new plant tribes.
Curling vines up high,
Forecast: Growth, oh my!

Dust bunnies take flight,
Chasing shadows at night.
Even cacti can laugh,
In their own prickly path.

Ferns wear feathery crowns,
Laughing with leafy gowns.
Our green friends adore,
Life's little uproar.

Nature's Lullaby

A gentle breath in,
Plants hum with a grin.
Wiggly worms below,
Conducting nature's show.

Sunbeams twinkle bright,
They dance with all their might.
My rubber plant sways,
To the sun's warm rays.

Whispers float through air,
Leaves gossip everywhere.
In every cracked pot,
Funny tales begot.

Growth in the Living Room

Green buddies in pots,
Spilling beans, like hot shots.
Limber limbs stretch wide,
In this leafy ride.

Candles flicker close,
While the garden boasts.
They wear my old shirts,
Fashionistas in flirts.

Cacti roll their eyes,
At the other guys.
Here we glow and grow,
Laughing in the show.

Cultivating Calm

In the corner, green,
Potting soil on my shoes.
A sneaky cat lurks,
They think it's a litter box.

Sunlight spills like juice,
Leaves dance in morning warmth.
I talk to my ferns,
They just wave back at me!

Watering can spills,
Oops! It's a garden party.
My plants throw confetti,
Moss is the guest of honor!

I try to be zen,
But forget my repotting.
Lively jungle laughs,
Tomorrow's another chance!

Tendrils of Time

Time moves slower here,
Worms wiggle with delight.
My chili plant sighs,
"Why do you eat my fruit?"

Ticking clock above,
It reminds me I'm late.
My cactus looks smug,
"Prickly but still a friend!"

Pothos drapes like silk,
A twist in every corner.
I've lost the scissors,
My plants now wear a scarf.

A leaf here, a leaf there,
Life's little messes grow tall.
I laugh at their joy,
Nature's silly surprise show!

The Art of Care

Growing plants indoors,
Is like a comedy show.
Each sprout tells a joke,
Watch it bloom with a grin!

Plant food resembles soup,
I sprinkle yours, not mine.
"Don't eat the last leaf!"
"Just a taste," giggles thyme.

Repotting's a dance,
Soil flies, we all tumble.
With glee, I declare,
"Next time, less enthusiasm!"

Little pots of joy,
Every leaf plays a part.
In this leafy play,
Nature's humor, my heart!

Unfolding Life

In a tiny pot,
Plants stretch as if to say,
"I could use some sun."
They invite me to stay.

Sprouts unfurl like jokes,
Leafy punchlines on display.
Every green leaf laughs,
At my gardening mistakes.

Banana peel mulch,
Who knew it could attract flies?
I sigh and I laugh,
"Guess they wanted a snack!"

In this wild garden,
We flirt with dirt and giggles.
Life unfolds with zest,
In our chaotic pot show!

Homegrown Whispers

In a pot so small,
A cactus thinks it's tough,
"I'm armed with sharp spikes!"
Yet it fears the cold.

Fern leaves waving cheer,
Throwing shade like a diva,
Talks to the spider:
"Get off my turf, friend!"

Succulent stash grows,
Hiding snacks for late-night snacks,
"It's just for me, yeah!"
In the fridge it snores.

Basil dreams of pasta,
Whispers of marinara,
All this fame and cook,
But still, it's just a sprout.

Windowsill Wonders

Tiny pots align,
A parade of green soldiers,
Guarding a sunbeam,
With grins made of leaves.

Alfred the Aloe,
Says hi to the passing cat,
"Don't chew on my tips!"
"Aloe, we must chat."

The ivy climbs high,
In search of a better view,
Yells "Look at me now!"
While falling from grace.

Pothos takes a leap,
Stretching out for more sunlight,
"Can I borrow yours?"
The curtain laughs back.

Nourished by Sunlight

Sunny side up leaf,
Eating rays like pancakes, yum!
"Life is pretty sweet,"
Said greens on a plate.

The daisy debates,
"Am I pretty or just bright?"
Reflects on the breeze,
Finding love in petals.

A rogue plant wanders,
Trying to find its way home,
Left on a table,
"Just one more minute, please!"

Orchid makes a fuss,
"Why does no one appreciate
My colors and grace?"
Petals in a huff.

Flora and Feelings

Pansy throws a fit,
"Everyone just passes me,"
Painted face in woe,
"Fame is fleeting, guys!"

Chives roll their green eyes,
"Why does thyme steal my thunder?
I'm tasty too, friend,"
A sassy herb truce.

Bromeliads whisper,
"Let's start a secret club,
For plants that feel shy,"
They giggle in leaves.

An avocado waits,
Wishing for a loyal hand,
"So close yet so far,"
"It's all about the toast!"

The Home within Green

In my sunny nook,
A fern talks to a chair,
Potted dreams whisper,
Who waters who today?

Succulent smiles beam,
Cacti raise their arms high,
"Don't poke my own eye!"
Laughter spreads like vines.

Leaves dance in the breeze,
Repotted for a laugh,
"Guess we're all growing!"
What's our new photograph?

My Aloe's got jokes,
Tells me when to chill out,
Keeps it cool and green,
Nature's smirking shout!

Tiny Forests

In a cup, they thrive,
Mini trees in a jar,
Each leaf a soft laugh,
Beneath a playful star.

Moss wears tiny hats,
Beans hopping 'round with glee,
"Join our tiny dance!"
Come join the jubilee!

Pinky-potted pals,
Throwing shade like they mean,
"We're the coolest crew, "
In a scene evergreen.

Teaspoon of sunshine,
Got a garden on a shelf,
Who needs vast old woods,
When I've got my own self?

Cornered Eden

Spiky friends in pots,
Swinging on their own ropes,
"Life's a spiky ride, "
Twisting with humor hopes.

One leaf says to the fern,
"I've got the shade today, "
Fern sighs and rolls eyes,
"You'd know if you could sway!"

Flower peeks from a nook,
Says, "I'm blooming bright now!"
Petals flaunt and laugh—
"Let's take a bold bow!"

In this vibrant space,
Laughter grows, it's bizarre,
From potted company,
We're wild like a backyard!

Echoes of Nature

Chatter from the leaves,
In tiny pots they sit,
Whispering their tales,
Full of mischief and wit.

A spider plant jokes,
"Who runs this green café?"
Got coffee in the air,
And snacks in clay soufflé.

Old snake plant winks,
"I'm tough, so take a look!"
My scars are battle marks,
In this lively nook.

Their laughter fills the room,
With roots that intertwine,
Nature's fun brigade,
Eager for sunshine!

Rooms of Respite

In the corner, green gang,
Plants all ponder, who shall hang?
Spider plant on the wall,
Whispers secrets, thinks it's tall.

Cactus winks, it feels quite slick,
Pointy friends are quite a trick.
Sunshine spills like lemonade,
On this leafy serenade.

Fern fronds wave in breezy dance,
Greenery gives a cheerful glance.
Chlorophyll dreams of the sun,
In this room, we're having fun.

Throw a towel on the floor,
Oops! Just stepped on limbs galore.
In this jungle of delight,
Plants and jokes take joyful flight.

Cultivated Joy

Potting soil, hands in glee,
Laughter rings of floral spree.
Watering can, not a chore,
Splashes joy right on the floor.

Succulent, prickly and proud,
Smirking under a leafy shroud.
Herb garden whispers to me,
'Basil knows the best of tea!'

Repotting brings a slight scare,
Roots all tangled, unaware.
Plant parade in my own yard,
Garden mischief, life's grand card.

With a sprinkle of delight,
My plants grow taller every night.
In the chaos I find peace,
Joy in every green release.

Leaves in Laughter

Bouncing leaves, a sprightly show,
Play along to nature's glow.
Foliage tickles, what a sight,
Dancing softly in the light.

Pothos plays peekaboo, sly,
Climbing high, it aims to fly.
In one pot, a party blooms,
Who knew plants had so much room?

Tiny sprouts are in a race,
Who will win this leafy chase?
Every branch has its own joke,
Laughter shared, no need to poke.

Nature's laughter fills the air,
Funny faces everywhere.
Witty roots and playful vines,
In this garden, joy aligns.

Nature's Palette

Canvas green, splashed with flair,
Colors bright, without a care.
Yellow blooms wink at the blue,
Nature's jokes in every hue.

Pot of gold, a daisy grin,
Laughs as petals spin and spin.
Sunshine smiles, oh, what a sight,
Painting dreams in morning light.

Leaves like clowns, all dressed up tight,
Jokes and jests from day to night.
Every corner a delight,
Garden parties feel so right.

Ripened fruits have things to say,
Swaying softly, bright display.
In this palette, we all play,
Nature's humor, come what may.

Nature's Inside Embrace

In a pot so round,
A cactus wears a frown.
Too much water, oh dear!
Next time, I'll just cheer.

Leafy friends at play,
Dancing all night, hooray!
Spinning on the shelf,
Maybe they can help?

A fern whispers low,
'Where did my sunlight go?'
I promised it bright rays,
But forgot on busy days.

Succulent so sweet,
Thinks it's a tasty treat.
Pulled the dog's attention,
It now needs intervention!

Leafy Love Letters

Letters from the vine,
'Can I have some wine?'
They sip from the dew,
And laugh at me too.

Each leaf a new tale,
Of wind, sun, and hail.
A plant friend of mine,
Scribbles on a vine.

Musty soil and roots,
Fashion trendy boots.
The plants had a ball,
With snacks and a brawl.

Postcards from each sprout,
'The garden's in a rout!'
They party and prance,
While I just glance.

Whispers of Green

Whispering leaves chat,
'Is that Mom's old hat?'
Soaked in sunshine's gleam,
  Their gossip is supreme.

Pot of gold, they say,
Can I take it to play?
Nursing dreams of fame,
  Or just a silly game?

A snake plant feels shy,
'Talk to me, oh my!'
Its long, leafy grin,
  Hides secrets within.

Watering can sighs,
'Why do they love flies?'
But sprays with delight,
  Frogs' parties at night!

Sunlight's Embrace

Sunlight creeping in,
'Oh boy, where to begin?'
Chasing rays around,
In the soil, they're found.

Curtains parted wide,
Plants all beam with pride.
Photosynthesizing,
While the cat is spying.

A rubber plant's grin,
'Another day to win!'
It stretches to the light,
Feeling oh so bright.

Yet a leaf did droop,
'Why am I in this loop?'
Pretending to be spry,
While wishing to fly.

Leafy Conversations

In the corner, green
Sipping sun like fine tea,
"You're taller than me!"
"Not if you stand on your leaves!"

Potted neighbor shouts,
"Keep your secrets to stems!"
"I have a wild dream,"
"Of sprouting a cat next week!"

Sunbeams spark the chat,
Photosynthesis jokes fly,
"I'm more of a star!"
"At least you're never dry!"

Congregation grows,
Sassy blooms joining the fun,
"May I borrow shade?"
"Only if you share water!"

Growth in Silence

In stillness, we thrive,
Whispers of roots in the dark,
All secrets we keep,
Our world beneath the pot.

Leaves listen closely,
To the gossip of raindrops,
"Did you hear the news?"
"The sun's coming out soon!"

Dust bunnies gather,
Underneath our leafy friends,
"Have you seen the dust?"
"Shall we start a clean team?"

Eavesdropping squirrels,
Pop their heads in for a look,
"What's cooking down here?"
"Just thoughts of us blooming!"

Nature's Gentle Hold

Gentle hugs of green,
A rubber plant goes viral,
"I'm so Instagram,"
"Just a leaf in your feed!"

A cactus rolls eyes,
As friends overflow with cheer,
"I'm prickly and tough!"
"But we love your spiky side!"

The herbs chat away,
"Who stole the basil this week?"
"I'm smelling a thief!"
"That tomato's too saucy!"

Budding blossoms grin,
"What if we throw a party?"
"All bugs are invited!"
"And no slugs on the dance floor!"

Ferns and Flickering Light

Ferns sway in delight,
Bathed in shafts of golden warmth,
"Dancing in the breeze?"
"Or just trying to survive!"

Moss sprawls like a rug,
We invited it today,
"Is it happy here?"
"Let's not ask, let it vibe!"

Shadows play peekaboo,
As sunlight flickers bright,
"Are you in the mood?"
"For a waltz or just chill out?"

Garden grand soirée,
Every leaf with a good tale,
"Spin me a yarn, friend!"
"I'm only green, but wise!"

Eco-Invitations

Please come, my dear friend,
Join us for some sun!
The ferns have planned a bash,
They've even brought the fun!

Cacti in their corner,
Throwing needles like darts,
Succulents, still polite,
Who knew they had such hearts?

The soil's all a-mingle,
With stories from the roots,
While petunias gossip,
In floral, flowery suits!

So grab that little shovel,
And help us dig in deep,
Let's plant some wild ideas,
And watch the laughter leap!

Fronds and Friends

In the corner, a fern,
With fronds of finest green,
It sways like a dancer,
In sunshine's warm sheen.

A cactus pipes up loud,
"Prickly but so fun!"
The rubber plant rolls eyes,
"Let's not poke anyone!"

The pothos makes a joke,
"I'm hanging out tonight!"
The peace lily just sighs,
"Can we keep it polite?"

Together, they provide,
A party leafy bright,
With laughter all around,
In their green, cozy light!

Gentle Transitions

Oh, winter's chill arrives,
My leafy friend's all bare,
He whispers soft goodbyes,
As he sheds without care.

Spring brings in fresh beginnings,
Tiny buds leap and cheer,
"I'll dance in morning light!"
The change, it feels so near.

The blooms erupt with laughter,
As colors bright parade,
Even weeds join the chorus,
To celebrate the shade!

Through seasons they all flourish,
With antics none can stop,
In the dance of the cycles,
They rise and then they drop!

Leafy Confessions

Oh, leafy friend of mine,
What secrets do you hold?
I see your browning tips,
A tale there to be told.

"My leaves are just too lazy,
They nap more than they grow,
But when the light is right,
Oh, the stories they bestow!"

And what about the soil?
"Too rich, it makes me weak,
I thrive on little water,
Just don't make me too sleek!"

So let's embrace the chaos,
In our green, jumbled quests,
With laughter, dirt, and sunlight,
These plants are truly blessed!

Leafy Secrets

In the corner they dwell,
Whispering secrets well.
Too loud are the ferns,
Poking fun at my concerns.

Cacti boast of their might,
'We thrive on neglect,' they write.
While succulents play it cool,
'Water? Nah, we're no fool!'

Trailing vines, oh, so sly,
Swinging low, they ask why.
'Why this mess, what a sight!'
'We just wanted some light!'

Leafy crew, in their glee,
Laughing at my lack of spree.
In my home, a plant parade,
A verdant, green charade.

Serene Companions

Pothos hangs with flair,
Telling me not to care.
'You've got time, take a seat,'
Leafy friends can't be beat.

Orchids flaunt their showy bloom,
Making my heart feel the room.
'Don't fret about that stain,'
'We absorb all your pain!'

Spider plants dance in glee,
Swaying at my silly spree.
'Trim us back? What a joke!'
'More leaves, more fun,' they provoke.

In laughter we bask,
Plants and I, they love to bask.
Living in harmony here,
With my quirky plant cheer.

Dappled Shadows

In sun-kissed spots they hide,
With leafy arms spread wide.
'Hey, watch out for the cat!'
'He's more trouble than that!'

Ferns whisper tales of grace,
To the dust in this place.
'We've seen every shoe drop,'
'Can you make the mess stop?'

Calatheas spin and twirl,
'Dance, dear human, unfurl!'
'You lag behind these days,'
They tease me in leafy ways.

Dappled shadows, they play,
Wit like sunbeams all day.
In this jungle I roam,
Laughing at my little home.

Roots of Resilience

Deep down in the earth they plot,
The secret of the pot.
'We thrive in messy dirt,'
'And that's how we assert!'

Roots tangled in a chase,
'Life's chaos? It's our space!'
They weave a sturdy game,
In this plant-life fame.

Sunshine? Sure, they will bask,
But hydration? Such a task!
Adventures truly grand,
'Oh, look, we've made a band!'

Roots of joy and laughter spread,
With every leaf and thread.
In this home where they grow,
Funny tales in every show.

Growth in Stillness

In a pot I sit,
Watching you rush by,
Got roots down deep,
But still feel shy.

Water me with care,
I'll stretch toward the sun,
Talk to me with flair,
Let's have some fun!

You say I'm low maintenance,
But I have needs, you know?
A dance with the sunlight,
And then I'll steal the show.

So here's my little secret,
I thrive on your attention,
Just don't spill the beans,
Or I'll need a suspension!

Nature's Quiet Haven

In my leafy kingdom,
I rule the green domain,
You sweep and vacuum,
I just feel no pain.

Your furry friends come sniff,
With curious delight,
I play it calm and stiff,
While they plot their night.

So lend me a warm smile,
And whisper sweet decree,
Nature's 'quiet haven'
Is the perfect place for me!

Now, please don't look so sad,
When I drop a leaf or two,
It's just my way of saying,
"I'm still here, how about you?"

The Language of Leaves

My leaves sway and whisper,
In the softest breeze,
Speaking in green tones,
With effortless ease.

You think I'm just silent,
A background in the room,
But I'll tell you secrets,
If you create some gloom.

Stand still, hold your breath,
And listen for my tale,
A tale of growth and laughter,
In the calm, I prevail.

So let's share a giggle,
In my chlorophyll chat,
For growing in silence,
Is where it's truly at!

Petals and Purpose

A sprout with great ambition,
Peeking from the dirt,
I gaze at your confusion,
While trying not to flirt.

In my pot, I ponder,
Life's challenges, so bright,
Petals on a journey,
To stretch and reach for light.

Oh, to be a cactus,
With spines, cool and chic,
With every single prick,
I'd surely cause a squeak!

So water me with kindness,
And we shall bloom in sync,
To plant our little jokes,
In the soil of pinky pink!

www.ingramcontent.com/pod-product-compliance
Lightning Source LLC
Chambersburg PA
CBHW072133070526
44585CB00016B/1653